Sheridan Coates

TECHNOLOGY:
BLUEPRINTS OF THE FUTURE™

TECHNOLOGY: BLUEPRINTS OF THE FUTURE™

Bullet Trains

Inside and Out

by
David Biello

Illustrations
Alessandro Bartolozzi
Roberto Simoni

The Rosen Publishing Group's
PowerPlus Books™
New York

For my cousin Erik

Published in 2002 in North America
by The Rosen Publishing Group, Inc., New York

First Edition

Book Design:
Andrea Dué s.r.l. Florence, Italy

Illustrations:
Alessandro Bartolozzi and Roberto Simoni

Editors and Photo Researchers:
Jason Moring and Joanne Randolph

Library of Congress Cataloging-in-Publication Data

Biello, David.
Bullet trains : inside and out / by David Biello. — 1st ed.
p. cm. — (Technology—blueprints of the future)
Includes bibliographical references and index.
ISBN 0-8239-6113-3 (library binding)
1. High speed trains—Juvenile literature. 2. Railroads—Trains.
[1. High speed trains. 2. Railroads—Trains.] I. Title. II. Series.
TF1450.B54 2002
385'.2—dc21
2001000871
Manufactured in Italy by Eurolitho S.p.A., Milan

Contents

High-Speed Travel and You   6

Some Railroad History   8

High-Speed Trains   10

High-Speed Technology   12

Brake and Track Technology   14

Development of the Shinkansen   16

Shinkansen Technology   18

Shinkansen Paves the Way   20

Train à Grande Vitesse   22

TGV Expands   24

TGV Technology   26

InterCity Express   28

ICE Technology   30

Tilting Trains   32

More on Tilting Trains   34

Acela   36

Other High-Speed Lines and Worldwide Projects   38

High-Speed Trains of the Future—Maglev   40

High-Speed Trains of the Future—Aerotrain   42

Glossary   44
Additional Resources   46
Index   47
About the Author/Credits   48

High-Speed Travel and You

Imagine traveling on a cushion of air, on a magnetic levitation train, at 300 mph (483 km/h)! You may soon be able to do that in some countries. For several years now, in Europe and Japan, "high-tech" steel-wheel electric trains have made routine trips of nearly 200 mph (321.8 km/h). As if that's not amazing enough, these countries have begun researching the possibility of "mag-lev" trains that will travel even faster all without touching the rails. How did we achieve this?

People have always traveled, even in ancient times. At first people traveled by foot, by riding on animals, by small boat, or, later, by riding in carriages pulled by animals. As centuries went by, sailing ships extended man's travel across oceans. Trade and warfare with other regions, and the need to move people to new and better areas to live, all propelled these new travel technologies. Nearly two hundred years ago, people began to travel by train. Train travel brought people together from great distances. However, it was eventually replaced in popularity by cars and airplanes.

In the last twenty to thirty-five years, development of modern high speed trains, spearheaded by Japan, has created a passenger railroad revival, as a much-needed alternative to crowded roads and airports. Europe and Japan, in particular, have used high-speed passenger trains, or "bullet trains," to move a lot of people quite successfully. The United States has lagged behind due to Americans' preference for cars over all other forms of transportation, but even in North America, several bullet train projects are being considered, or launched, such as Acela in the Northeast Corridor of the United States.

If you are interested in train travel, this is one of the most exciting times to be alive. Train travel remained pretty much the same for most of history, but recently scientists, engineers, and researchers have been coming up with all kinds of different ideas for how to make trains faster, cleaner, and safer. We achieved all of this because human beings like to solve problems. You will find in this book that when roads got crowded, people built better trains. When there were problems with old train technology, new train technology was created. The rise of the bullet train is just one of many examples of how we use technology to create a new and better future for the world to come.

John F. Shields
Executive Director
SPEEDTRAIN
Californians for High Speed Passenger Rail

Right: As the population has grown, the roads have become increasingly congested. Many people have begun to look for another, more convenient way to travel. This method in many places is the high-speed train.

Right: This is a Japanese Shinkansen, or bullet train. The train here is a Nozomi 500 model, one of the fastest trains in the world.

祝 700系の

Some Railroad History

The very first railroads were built to make it easier to transport metals and coal from mines. Because of the lack of technology and the great weight of these products, the process of moving this freight remained slow and difficult.

In an effort to solve this problem, Great Britain's Richard Trevithick built the first steam-powered locomotive in 1803. The locomotive, the *New Castle*, was slow and heavy, and was used only to move very heavy freight.

By 1829, however, Englishman George Stephenson had developed a more lightweight engine, the *Rocket*, which was the prototype for all future steam engines. Such engines, and the new railroads they required, spread throughout the world as a cheap and an effective way to move people and products from place to place. By the 1900s, steam locomotives were capable of moving freight trains at speeds up to 75 mph (121 km/h). These engines were easy to use and long lasting, but they also produced a lot of pollution and eventually ruined the rails because of the pounding motion of the piston driving the crank.

As early as 1835, engineers experimented with using electricity instead of steam to power locomotives, but it was not until 1879 that the German company Siemens & Halske unveiled the first working electric locomotive. Because electrical engines were so simple, they needed less maintenance and lasted even longer than did steam engines. However, in order to run they required a lot of electricity. Because the systems of wires and generators necessary to power them were so complicated, they were not practical for long-distance use.

As a result, a better, more practical locomotive was needed. Dr. Rudolf Diesel patented the diesel engine in 1892. By the 1920s, diesel-electric locomotives were produced. In these locomotives, a diesel engine ran a generator that produced the electricity for the electric motors of the train. By the end of the 1930s, diesel-electric passenger and freight trains had replaced steam engines throughout much of the world, and they are still in use today.

As time went on, however, airplanes began to be used for long-distance trips and automobiles for shorter ones. Passengers began demanding greater speed and

Right: This is a memorial to George Stephenson.

Below: The *Rocket* became the prototype for all future steam engines. The great force of escaping steam drove a piston linked to the wheels, causing them to turn and move the train.

Left: When George Stephenson, pictured here, sent the first steam-powered passenger train down the tracks at 16 miles per hour, or mph (26 km/h), in 1825, he hardly could have imagined that only 139 years later bullet trains would average speeds of 130 mph (209 km/h). Today high-speed trains in development actually fly down the tracks at speeds of more than 300 mph (483 km/h) without even touching the rails.

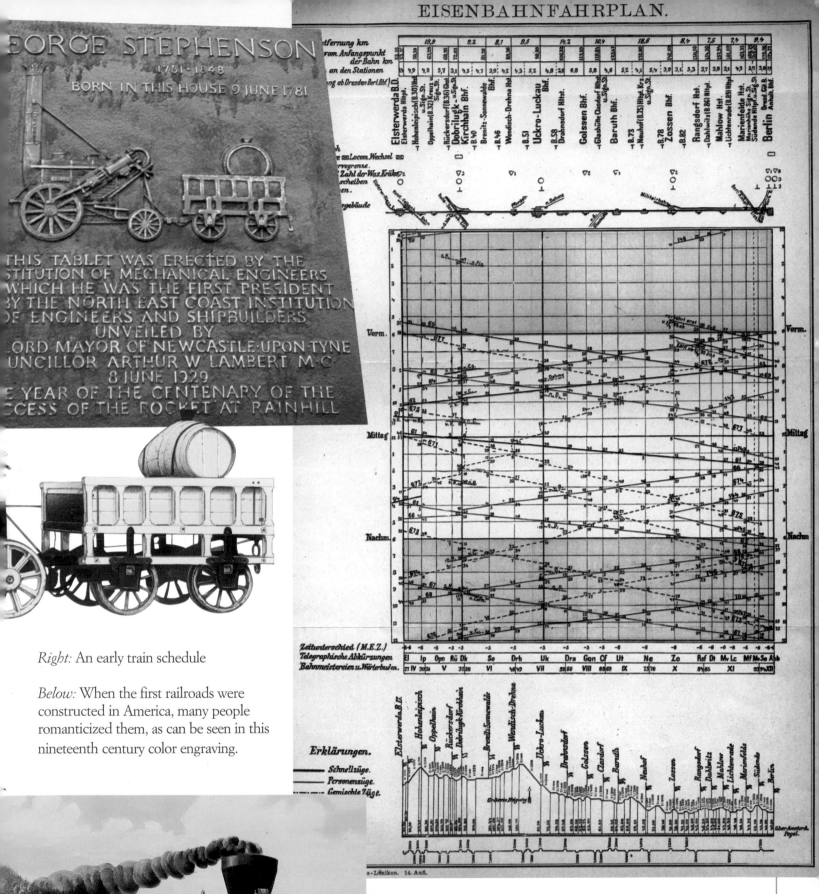

GEORGE STEPHENSON
1781-1848
BORN IN THIS HOUSE 9 JUNE 1781

THIS TABLET WAS ERECTED BY THE
INSTITUTION OF MECHANICAL ENGINEERS
OF WHICH HE WAS THE FIRST PRESIDENT
AND BY THE NORTH EAST COAST INSTITUTION
OF ENGINEERS AND SHIPBUILDERS
UNVEILED BY
THE LORD MAYOR OF NEWCASTLE-UPON-TYNE
COUNCILLOR ARTHUR W LAMBERT M·C·
8 JUNE 1929
THE YEAR OF THE CENTENARY OF THE
SUCCESS OF THE ROCKET AT RAINHILL

Right: An early train schedule

Below: When the first railroads were
constructed in America, many people
romanticized them, as can be seen in this
nineteenth century color engraving.

convenience from railroads, and those that could not
provide it, like many passenger railroads in the United
States, went out of business. It seemed as if the passenger railroad soon would be a thing of the past, like
travel on horseback.

High-Speed Trains

It took Japanese engineering to keep railroads from losing all passenger traffic. In 1964, the Japanese introduced the world's first high-speed train—what would become known as the bullet train. The train got its name from the distinctive shape of its nose, which made it resemble a bullet as it sped down the track. This rounded, smooth shape allowed the train to move more quickly and quietly than did less aerodynamic trains.

The Japanese name for the bullet train, Shinkansen, which translates as "new trunk line" in English, came from the fact that an entirely new system of rails, or trunk lines, had to be built to allow the new trains to travel so fast. When trains travel around curves at high speeds, gravity pushes passengers into their seats. To avoid this uncomfortable effect, workers laid long, welded steel rails in as straight a line as possible.

The bullet train was an instant success with the Japanese traveler. Today bullet trains run throughout Japan, connecting cities in every part of the country. In fact, almost 300 trains run daily and the trains carry more than 300 million passengers every year.

Inspired by the success of the Shinkansen, the French began construction of their own high-speed railway in the 1970s. After a decade of testing, the Train à Grande Vitesse (TGV), which translates literally as "train of great speed," made its first trip with passengers in 1981 at a maximum operating speed of 168 mph (270 km/h). Its speedy success prompted the French to build even faster TGV lines throughout France.

Soon high-speed trains, trains traveling 120 mph (193 km/h) or faster, had spread throughout the world, providing an alternative to polluting car and plane travel. For example, Germany has the InterCity Express (ICE), created in the 1980s. It became a dedicated high-speed rail service in 1991. These trains can travel at speeds up to 174 mph (280 km/h). Countries

Trains powered by diesel are still in use today, but high-speed rail lines are faster, cleaner, and more convenient for rail passengers.

A diesel motor
for trains

like Spain, Switzerland, and the United States also have high-speed trains. Not every country has a dedicated high-speed line the way Japan, France, or Germany does, but these other countries have adapted high-speed technology for use on standard rail lines.

Now let's take a look at the technology that allows these high-speed trains to work, as well as the various types of high-speed trains throughout the world.

French TGV rail yard

High-Speed Technology

All high-speed trains, from the Japanese Shinkansen to the French TGV, rely on advanced technology to travel so fast. From the motors that run the trains to the brakes that stop them, special equipment had to be designed and built to make these high-speed trains practical and safe.

The first step was building a more powerful engine. Originally diesel fuel powered the Japanese Shinkansen, but, in order to protect the environment and cut down on the use of oil, almost all modern high-speed trains run on pure electrical power. These new electric engines produce far less pollution and use less energy than did the older diesel ones.

To achieve the amount of power necessary to run a train at high speeds, engineers installed electric motors on each axle, or the shaft around which the wheel turns, of a train. The axle is firmly attached to two wheels to form a wheelset. Two wheelsets are then mounted in a bogie, which is a rigid frame that connects and surrounds two separate wheelsets. On a Japanese Shinkansen train, two motorized bogies provide the forward motion for each individual car. French TGV train cars actually are connected and propelled by shared motorized bogies.

The electric motors on the bogies get their power from the engines attached at either end of most high-speed trains. Instead of a diesel engine powering a generator, on modern trains a pantograph attaches to an overhead catenary, or a wire carrying an electrical current. This power in the catenary is at a high voltage so that it can travel the distances between generating stations and so that less power is lost as it travels down the wire. A transformer in the engine reduces the power coming in from the catenary to the right voltage for the electric motors in the bogies. The transformer also completes the circuit with the power supply by sending the remaining energy back into the tracks through the axle brush.

The proper voltage is then sent from the transformer to the individual motors in the bogies. This power turns the motor, which turns the axle, which turns the wheel, which sends the train down the tracks. This system has been used to reach speeds of more than 300 mph (483 km/h).

In order for these electric trains to achieve truly high speeds without derailing or causing passenger discomfort, new rails need to be laid that are as straight as possible. Workers use long, welded pieces of steel rail for this purpose. To keep the tracks straight, the ground itself also often has to be flattened by moving the earth aside; or else bridges, tunnels, or viaducts have to be built.

Right, top: This is a labeled diagram of a modern bogie design, which provides power to the wheels and thereby moves the train. The bogie, or truck as it is often called in the United States, comes in many shapes and sizes but the most advanced is the motor bogie of an electric or diesel locomotive. A motor bogie has to carry the motors, brakes, and suspension systems all within a small mechanism. It is subjected to huge stresses, especially in a high-speed train.

Right, bottom: A high-speed train travels across a bridge that was built specially for high-speed rail service.

Bogie

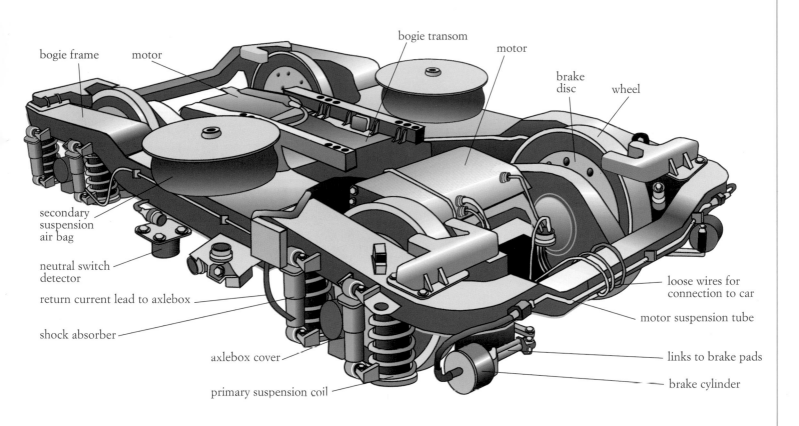

bogie frame   motor   bogie transom

motor

brake disc   wheel

secondary suspension air bag

neutral switch detector

return current lead to axlebox

shock absorber

axlebox cover

primary suspension coil

loose wires for connection to car

motor suspension tube

links to brake pads

brake cylinder

Brake and Track Technology

The long rails are laid on sleepers or ties that are made from concrete and steel. Regular trains use wooden ties but these would not keep a bullet train stable at high speeds. The long, welded tracks resting on concrete ties used for high-speed trains are called slabtrack and allow passengers to travel at high speeds without feeling as if they are moving at all.

Right: A bullet train speeds past Japanese workers in a rice paddy.

One unfortunate side effect of these stronger ties is that the concrete reflects all the noise of the passing trains. The concrete is harder and denser than wood so the sound of passing trains bounces off it into the surrounding area, much like the roar of traffic on a highway. This can be very loud, especially if you live in Japan near one of the Shinkansen lines where trains pass every six minutes.

While the French use shared bogies to link trains, couplers link high-speed trains in the rest of the world. Shaped like knuckles, these couplers automatically link up when the two train cars are pushed together. This allows high-speed railroad workers to attach or remove extra cars quickly and easily.

In addition, special brakes had to be developed so that the high-speed trains could stop without damaging either their wheels or the rails. Ordinary train brakes, which involve pressing a pad against the wheels, would cause a high-speed train to skid to a stop. This way of braking also produces a lot of heat that could melt the wheels, the rails, or even the brakes themselves and make it unsafe for the train to continue on its journey. Instead, most modern

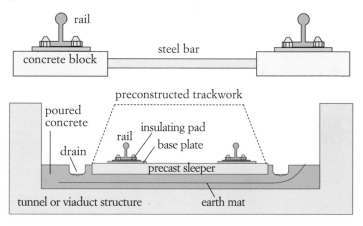

TWIN BLOCK TRACK

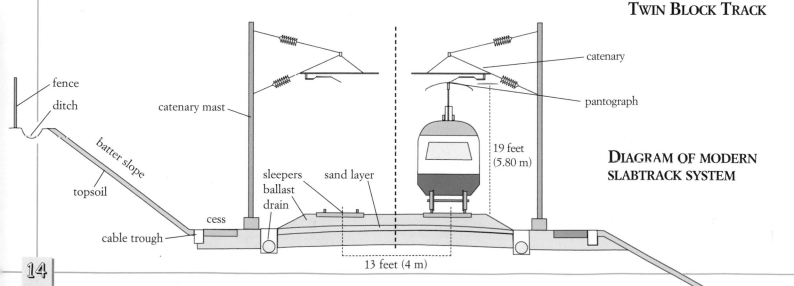

DIAGRAM OF MODERN SLABTRACK SYSTEM

high-speed trains are equipped with special dynamic brakes. When the brakes are applied, the traction motors already attached to the wheels stop moving and the forward motion of the train begins to move the wheels in the opposite direction. Because the motors are hard to turn, they slow down the train. In the process, they also turn the stopping motion of the train back into energy. Once the train has slowed down, pneumatic brakes are used to bring it to a complete stop. The energy generated by the traction motors during braking then can be turned into heat and radiated through grills with cooling fans. This is called rheostatic braking.

The energy also can be fed back into the circuit and used when the train starts up again. This is called regenerative braking. The most advanced high-speed trains are capable of either rheostatic or regenerative braking depending on how much current is already in the catenary.

Because the trains travel at such high speeds, it is impossible for the driver to see and react to the old system of trackside signals that indicate when to slow down or speed up. Instead most high-speed trains receive electrical signals from a central control station through the tracks themselves. This central computer feeds electrical signals into the rails, a computer onboard the high-speed train picks up the signals and then translates them into instructions for the driver. For example, the appropriate speed for a section of track as well as any maintenance or traffic information will be displayed to a TGV or a Shinkansen driver upon entering that section.

Left, middle: Pictured is a diagram of a twin block track using the modern slabtrack system, which is pictured below it.

Left, bottom: This is a modern slabtrack system. Slabtrack is used by most of the high-speed trains in the world because it increases safety and reduces maintenance. Regular ballast tracks break down due to the vibration of the train and have to be replaced each night. Slabtrack eliminates this problem and provides for a smoother ride.

Development of the Shinkansen

In 1959, after more than a decade of debate, a Japanese government panel, convinced by the expert testimony of Shinji Sogo, then president of Japanese National Railways, decided to build an entirely new system of tracks to carry high-speed trains. The new shinkansen lines would run alongside and largely replace the old, narrow-gauge railroad system. Only five-and-a-half years later, on October 1, 1964, the Tokaido shinkansen line between Tokyo and Osaka was completed.

The Japanese decided to build the new high-speed railroad between Tokyo and Osaka to lessen the overcrowding of already existing railroads and highways. Named after the ancient Tokaido path connecting Tokyo and the west coast of Japan, the Tokaido megalopolis stretches from Tokyo to Osaka and includes the cities of Yokohama, Kawasaki, Kyoto, and Nagoya. It contains 40 percent of Japan's population, or more than 50 million people. The very first Japanese railroad was built in this area in 1872, but by 1960, the best travel time between Tokyo and Osaka remained a slow 6 hours and 30 minutes.

The Japanese designed the Tokaido Shinkansen line to speed up that trip. First a new line of long, welded steel rails without any sharp curves was laid to allow trains to run at speeds of 150 mph (241 km/h). To make the tracks as straight as possible, the Tokaido Shinkansen required the construction of more than 40 miles (64 km) of tunnels, 11 miles (18 km) of bridges, and 28 miles (45 km) of viaducts. The tracks were laid on concrete ties to reduce train vibrations.

Right: Of all the Japanese Shinkansen models, Nozomi 500 trains are some of the fastest and most modern. The type is distinguished by its long nose, giving it an extremely aerodynamic profile. The driver's cab has a dome window, to allow excellent forward vision. The 500 Series also uses an innovative pantograph design, shaped like a wing, which helps reduce wind resistance. Extensive soundproofing means there is little sensation of speed inside trains, and wind noise is at a minimum.

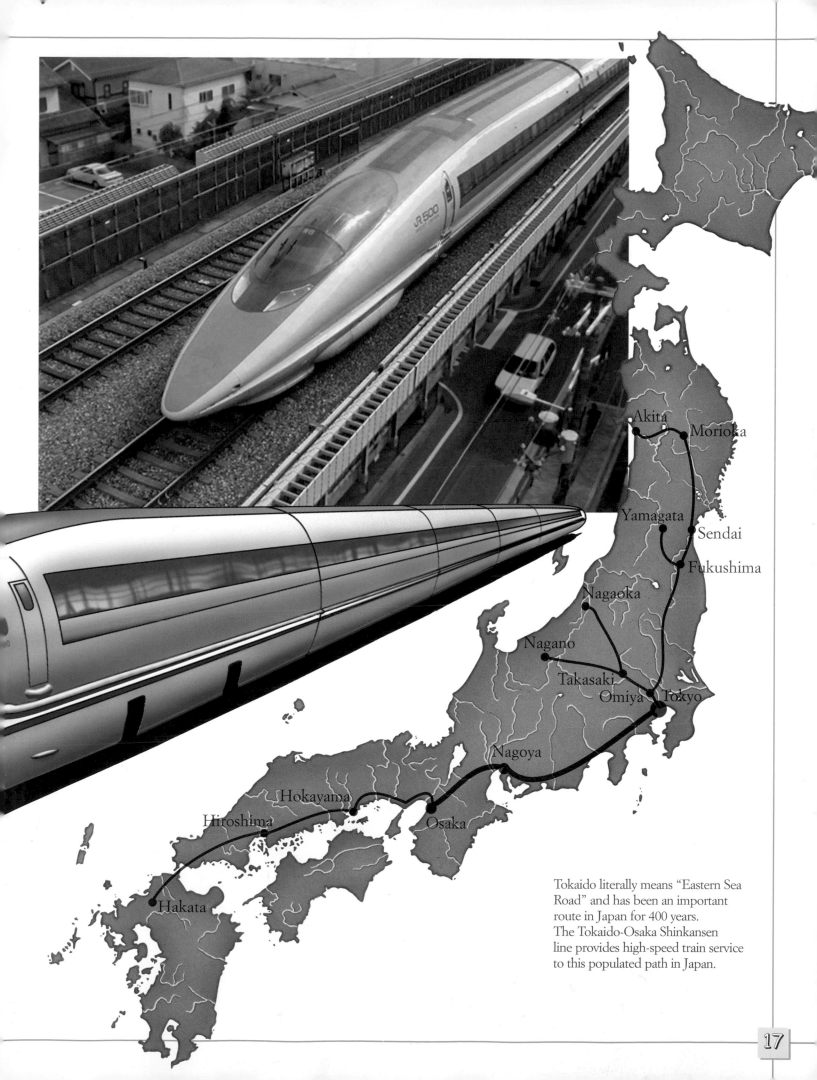

Akita
Morioka
Yamagata
Sendai
Fukushima
Nagaoka
Nagano
Takasaki
Omiya Tokyo
Nagoya
Hokayama
Hiroshima
Osaka
Hakata

Tokaido literally means "Eastern Sea Road" and has been an important route in Japan for 400 years. The Tokaido-Osaka Shinkansen line provides high-speed train service to this populated path in Japan.

Shinkansen Technology

While the construction of the tracks took place, engineers ran prototype trains on test tracks. These original Shinkansen vehicles were made of welded steel and were painted blue and white. On March 30, 1963, one of the prototypes set a world speed record for trains by traveling at 160 mph (257 km/h). The bullet train was ready for service.

Twelve cars made up the very first Shinkansen trains in service. Unlike an ordinary train, which is pulled by an engine at one end, each Shinkansen car had four axles with an electric motor. The whole train produced a total power of 6,624 horsepower. Originally a diesel engine ran a generator to provide the electricity for these electric motors. Soon, however, catenaries were strung alongside the track. A pantograph extended to the catenary from every other car to draw electric power for these motors. The engines at the front and rear of the train only carried the transformers that changed the electricity from the catenary into the power needed to turn the motors on each axle. The whole train without passengers weighed 672 tons (610 t).

From the beginning, all shinkansen trains also included an Automatic Train Control system that displayed braking control signals for the driver. Signals are sent and received through the track itself and come from the General Control Center in Tokyo. Controllers there still decide when, where, and how fast all the trains on all the Shinkansen lines will run at any given time. As a backup, all Shinkansen trains also are equipped with a radio telephone system.

All Shinkansen trains are air-conditioned, and the windows are sealed so that they cannot be opened. Because the trains travel so fast, designers installed a special ventilation system to make sure that the air pressure inside the trains remains the same throughout the trip. This is particularly important as the train passes through tunnels where a change in air pressure can result in passengers' ears popping uncomfortably.

The first Shinkansen trains became instantly popular because they cut travel time between Osaka and Tokyo from more than 6 hours to just over 3 hours when using the fastest trains. At first, only two trains—an express and a local, or train that made all sixteen stops—operated every hour, but heavy demand led to the frequency of train trips increasing every year. Even the local train was much faster than the old trains, making the trip in just four hours. Originally only 360 Shinkansen cars were built and used, but more were ordered quickly as the shinkansen line grew in success.

The only drawback to these trains was the noise they produced. Because of the high speeds and the special concrete ties that reflected all the noise, these Shinkansen trains could be very loud. To reduce the noise, sound-proof walls were built alongside the Shinkansen tracks. Heavier catenaries and aerodynamic pantographs have been designed also, but the Shinkansen are still loud. Researchers continue to find ways to make the trains quieter.

With the success of the Tokaido Shinkansen, officials planned more lines. In 1975, the Sanyo Shinkansen connected Osaka and Hakata to the west. Maximum speed on this line was planned for more than 160 mph (257 km/h), so the curves had to be reduced even more. With the opening of this line, passengers could travel from Tokyo to Hakata, almost 700 miles (1,127 km), in less than 7 hours.

In 1982, the Tohuku Shinkansen opened. It travels from outside Tokyo to Morioka in the far north of Japan. This line travels through 116 tunnels and 55 percent of it is built on viaducts as it passes through very mountainous and uneven countryside. It also travels through some very snowy regions, so trains on this line are built to keep out snow and cold. Hot-air devices, automatic snow-removing sprinklers, and hot water jets line the tracks to keep off snow and ice. Snowsheds are built over the exposed tracks to protect against avalanches.

Left: This is a cardboard model of the Japanese Nozomi 500 Shinkansen.

Shinkansen Paves the Way

In 1985, the Joetsu Shinkansen opened. It traveled from outside Tokyo to Niigata in the northwest. This line also traveled through a very mountainous region and 106 tunnels had to be built, including the Daishimizu tunnel. The Daishimizu is the world's longest railroad mountain tunnel; it stretches for almost 14 miles (23 km). This Shinkansen line was extended even farther to Nagano in time for the 1998 Winter Olympics.

Since the beginning of high-speed service in 1964, many different types of trains have been used on the lines. The original white and blue trains, called the 0 (Zero) series, remained in service until 1986 on the Sanyo Shinkansen. The more aerodynamic and lighter 100 series entered service on the Tokaido and Sanyo Shinkansen lines in 1985.

Series 0 Tokaido 1964

100 Tokaido 1980

200 Joetsu 1982

The white and green 200 series, designed for the snowy Tohuku and Joetsu lines, began service in 1982. The sleeker gray and green E1 "Max" trains replaced the 200 series in 1994. Today bright white, yellow, and blue E4 "Max" trains run at more than 170 mph (274 km/h) along the Tohuku line. The fastest Shinkansen trains run on the crowded Tokaido and Sanyo lines, where double-decker cars were introduced in 1985 to accommodate as many passengers as possible. The 100 series on this line was followed by the 300 and 400 series until, in 1992, the 500 series, called Nozomi, which means "hope" in Japanese, appeared with a top speed of almost 190 mph (306 km/h). In 1999, they were joined by the more aerodynamic and quieter Nozomi 700 series.

To reduce noise as much as possible, the Nozomi 500 and 700 series both have longer noses than did earlier Shinkansen trains. At 49 feet (15 m) they are three times as long as the original Zero series. This allows them to slice more smoothly through the air at high speeds. In addition, the pantographs are wing-shaped to minimize the amount of noise it creates. Both trains are made of lightweight aluminum instead of steel, and both are among the fastest high-speed trains currently running in the world.

Today, Japan is not the only country with high-speed rail service. Many other nations have followed Japan's lead and built high-speed rail lines. Throughout the world, high-speed trains have increased passengers' ability to travel quickly, conveniently, and cheaply. These high-speed railroads also disturb the natural environment far less than does a highway or an airport, and the high-speed trains themselves produce far less pollution than do either cars or planes while using less fuel. They are also an incredibly safe means of travel. In 1994, when the Shinkansen lines celebrated 30 years of operation, they could also celebrate the carrying of 2.8 billion passengers without a single serious injury. The same is true for the nearly 20 years the TGV has been in operation.

Below: These are many of the various Japanese Shinkansen designs that have been created since 1964. They are arranged in chronological order from left to right.

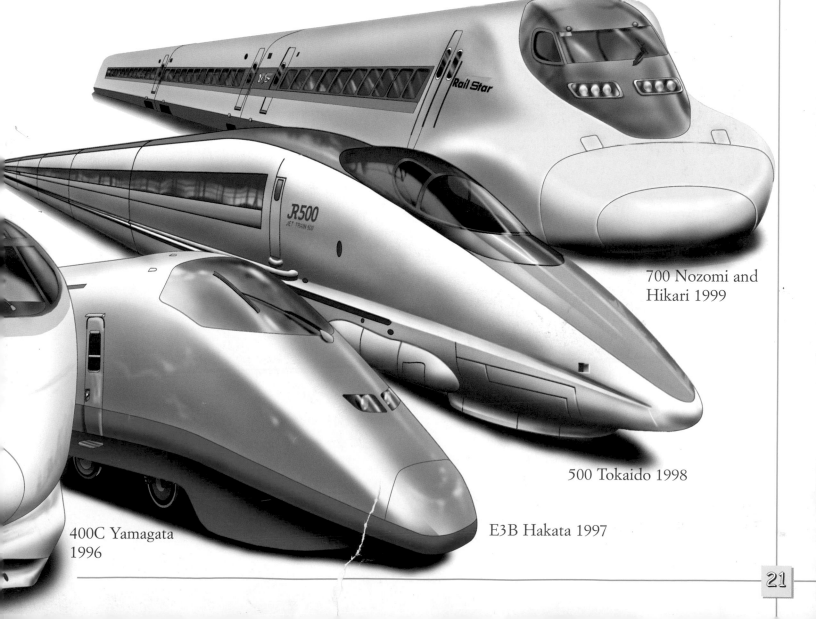

700 Nozomi and Hikari 1999

500 Tokaido 1998

E3B Hakata 1997

400C Yamagata 1996

Train à Grande Vitesse

Inspired by the Japanese, the Société Nationale des Chemins de Fer Français (SNCF), or the National French Railroad Society, began development of a high-speed railroad for France in the 1960s. The Train à Grande Vitesse (TGV) is not only the name of the trains they developed, but also of the track and signaling technology that allows high-speed train travel in France.

SNCF designers used a similar aerodynamic shape for their trains and concrete sleepers like those on the Japanese trains, but they also contributed several innovations of their own. From the beginning, SNCF officials wanted to develop a high-speed train that could run on existing tracks as well as on new high-speed lines. This decision to use the same gauge rails for high-speed tracks as was used on the regular tracks allowed the new high-speed trains to use the new tracks for high speed travel and to use the old tracks for entering and exiting major cities at slower speeds.

The first prototype train, the TGV 001, began testing in the early 1970s. Powered by a gas turbine, it set the world speed record in 1972 by reaching a speed of 198 mph (319 km/h). Like the Shinkansen, all of its axles were powered by electric motors, but in this case, the power for these motors came from gas turbines in the engine instead of a catenary or a diesel engine. The same type of long, welded, steel rails laid on concrete and steel ties were used for the tracks.

It quickly became apparent, however, that it would be too expensive to power the TGVs using gas, so, like the Shinkansen, electric engines were developed. In early 1981, an electric TGV reached a top speed of 236 mph (380 km/h). This TGV drew its power from an overhead catenary. A transformer located in the engine then changed the power from the catenary into the proper voltage to power the electric motors in each individual bogie.

The largest difference between the TGV and the Shinkansen bullet trains lies in the fact that the cars of the TGV are not coupled together but actually rest on a shared two-axle bogie. Sharing bogies makes the train lighter, allowing higher speeds, and also reduces the noise passengers hear when traveling to below that of a regular train. Because of the shared bogies, however, it is difficult to couple and uncouple extra cars, so sometimes two whole trains are linked to make particularly crowded trips.

Above: TGV trains wait in a station in Paris, France.

Below: The TGV Atlantique train was introduced in 1989.

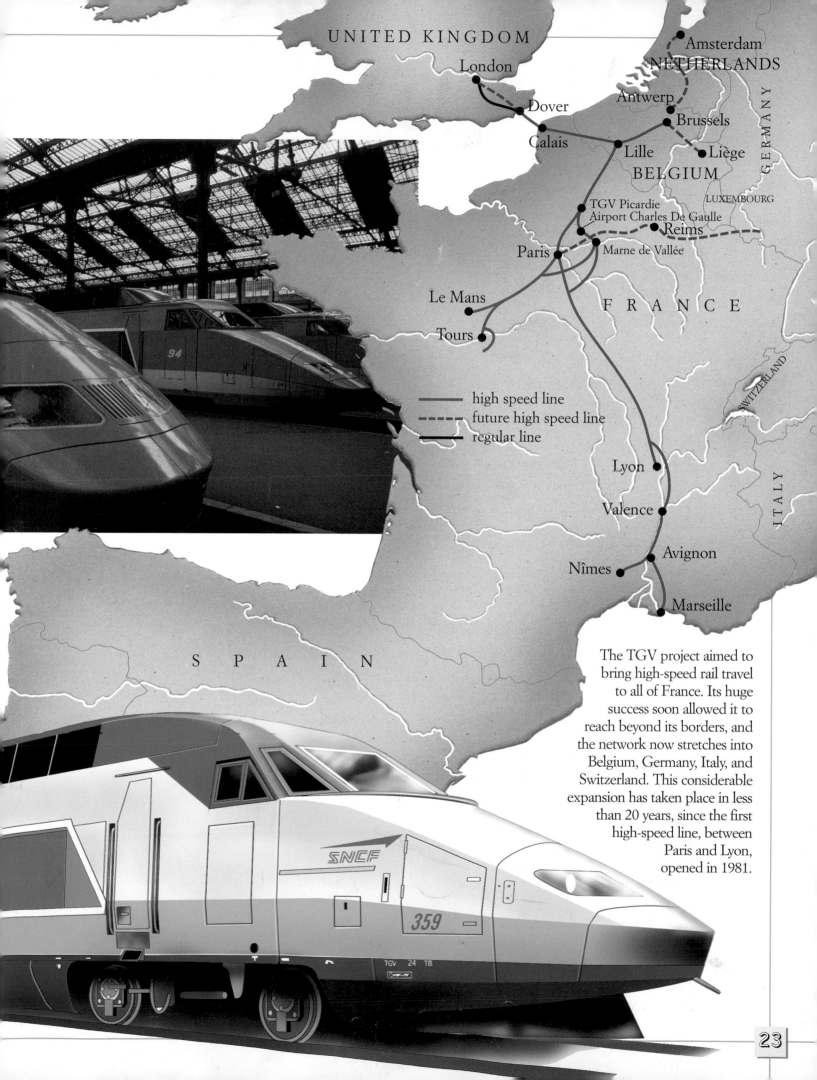

UNITED KINGDOM

London

Dover

Calais

Amsterdam

NETHERLANDS

Antwerp

Brussels

Lille

Liège

BELGIUM

GERMANY

LUXEMBOURG

TGV Picardie
Airport Charles De Gaulle

Reims

Paris

Marne de Vallée

Le Mans

F R A N C E

Tours

SWITZERLAND

high speed line

future high speed line

regular line

Lyon

Valence

ITALY

Avignon

Nîmes

Marseille

S P A I N

The TGV project aimed to
bring high-speed rail travel
to all of France. Its huge
success soon allowed it to
reach beyond its borders, and
the network now stretches into
Belgium, Germany, Italy, and
Switzerland. This considerable
expansion has taken place in less
than 20 years, since the first
high-speed line, between
Paris and Lyon,
opened in 1981.

SNCF

359

TGV 24 TB

TGV Expands

The first French high-speed tracks were built between Paris and Lyons, a distance of 241 miles (388 km). Catenaries ran alongside the tracks. They carried the 25,000 volts of electricity needed to power the train. Like the Shinkansen system, a control center transmitted all signals to the driver through the tracks. On entering any section of track, the driver could see the speed to be maintained as well as any special instructions. A special safety system to make sure that the driver has executed the signals was also installed. It automatically engaged the brakes if signals were not followed or if there was danger.

Below: This is a coupler. A coupler is the device that connects two train cars and allows them both to receive power, information about braking, and other mechanical information.

On September 27, 1981, the first passenger TGV, the TGV Sud-Est (TGV-SE), which means TGV "South East," left Paris for Lyons in the south of France. Like the Tokaido Shinkansen, it was an immediate success. Now sixty trains run in each direction every day, carrying an average of 53,000 passengers. The original TGV-SE could carry only 386 passengers, but new double-decker cars, introduced in 1997, can carry up to 545 passengers at speeds up to 186 mph (299 km/h). The TGV-SE line has more than 100 trains, each of which is made up of ten vehicles—an engine at each end and eight passenger cars.

With the success of the TGV-SE, a new line was built from Paris to cities along the Atlantic coast of France, the TGV Atlantique (TGV-A). Because the countryside between these regions was flatter, even higher speeds could be attained and special silver and blue trains were built for use on this line. A new air suspension system absorbed the vibrations produced by travel at speeds up to 190 mph (306 km/h). The trains were sealed with a special ventilation system, like the Japanese Shinkansen, to allow them to pass through tunnels without a change in air pressure. Two engines at the front and the back and ten passenger cars capable of carrying a total of 485 passengers made up each TGV-A train.

Left: The control panel of the TGV provides the conductor with information about train speed, transmission vibration, and similar data that ensure a smooth and safe trip.

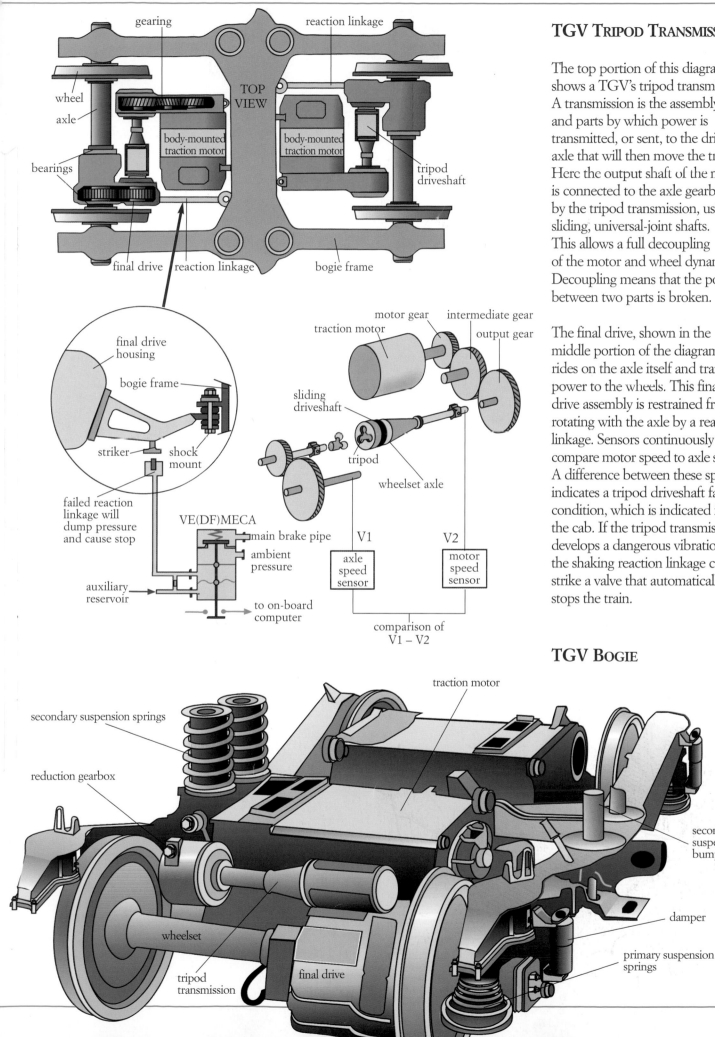

gearing

reaction linkage

TOP VIEW

wheel

axle

body-mounted traction motor

body-mounted traction motor

tripod driveshaft

bearings

final drive

reaction linkage

bogie frame

TGV TRIPOD TRANSMISSION

The top portion of this diagram shows a TGV's tripod transmission. A transmission is the assembly and parts by which power is transmitted, or sent, to the driving axle that will then move the train. Here the output shaft of the motor is connected to the axle gearbox by the tripod transmission, using sliding, universal-joint shafts. This allows a full decoupling of the motor and wheel dynamics. Decoupling means that the power between two parts is broken.

The final drive, shown in the middle portion of the diagram, rides on the axle itself and transfers power to the wheels. This final drive assembly is restrained from rotating with the axle by a reaction linkage. Sensors continuously compare motor speed to axle speed. A difference between these speeds indicates a tripod driveshaft failure condition, which is indicated in the cab. If the tripod transmission develops a dangerous vibration, the shaking reaction linkage can strike a valve that automatically stops the train.

final drive housing

bogie frame

sliding driveshaft

motor gear

intermediate gear

traction motor

output gear

striker

shock mount

tripod

wheelset axle

failed reaction linkage will dump pressure and cause stop

VE(DF)MECA

main brake pipe

ambient pressure

auxiliary reservoir

to on-board computer

V1

axle speed sensor

V2

motor speed sensor

comparison of V1 – V2

TGV BOGIE

secondary suspension springs

traction motor

reduction gearbox

secondary suspension bump stops

damper

wheelset

tripod transmission

final drive

primary suspension springs

TGV Technology

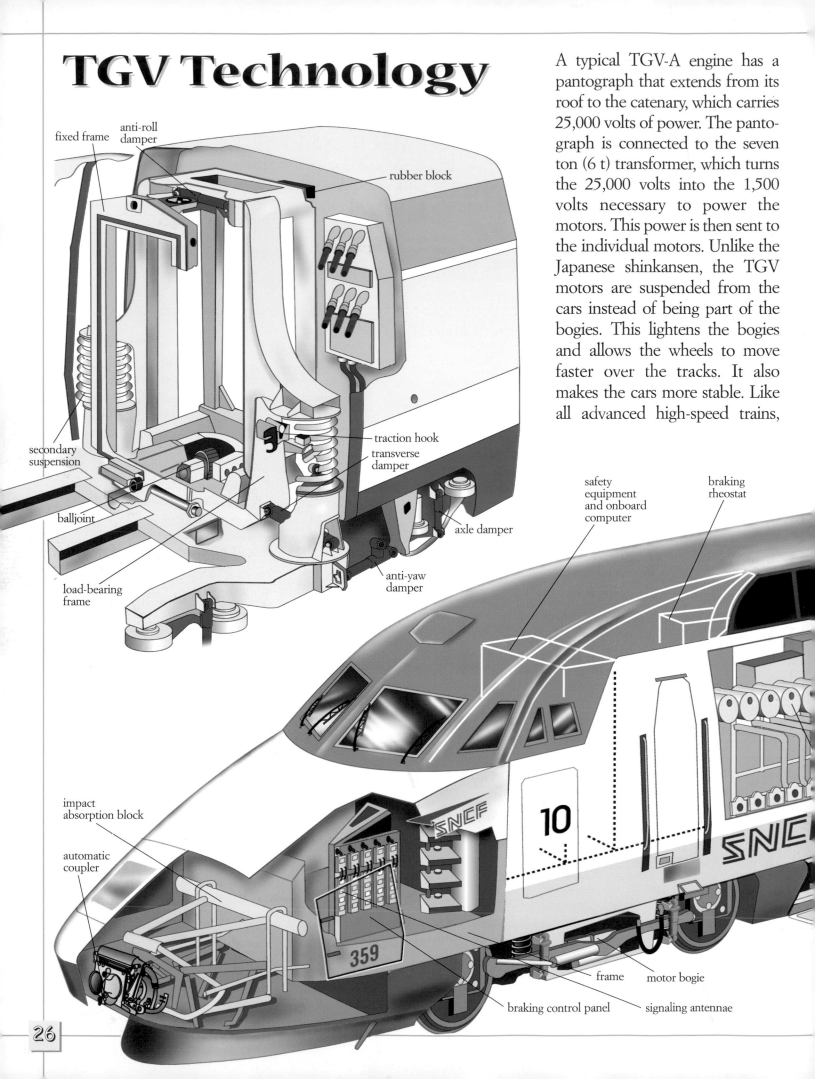

fixed frame

anti-roll
damper

rubber block

secondary
suspension

balljoint

load-bearing
frame

traction hook

transverse
damper

axle damper

anti-yaw
damper

A typical TGV-A engine has a pantograph that extends from its roof to the catenary, which carries 25,000 volts of power. The pantograph is connected to the seven ton (6 t) transformer, which turns the 25,000 volts into the 1,500 volts necessary to power the motors. This power is then sent to the individual motors. Unlike the Japanese shinkansen, the TGV motors are suspended from the cars instead of being part of the bogies. This lightens the bogies and allows the wheels to move faster over the tracks. It also makes the cars more stable. Like all advanced high-speed trains,

safety
equipment
and onboard
computer

braking
rheostat

impact
absorption block

automatic
coupler

SNCF

10

SNCF

359

frame

motor bogie

braking control panel

signaling antennae

TGVs are equipped with dynamic brakes, and sensors decide whether to feed the energy produced by braking back into the catenary or to radiate it as heat.

On May 18, 1990, a TGV-A train set a world speed record of 321 mph (517 km/h), or about half the speed of an airplane, thanks to the train's lightweight construction and more powerful and efficient electric motors. Although this high speed is impressive and useful for the information gathered on reaching such high speeds, it is still not practical for high-speed trains to travel this fast during regular service. Still, research continues into TGV Nouvelle Génération (TGV-NG), or "New Generation," technology that would permit passenger trains to run between 218 and 249 mph (351–401 km/h).

TGV lines also have been extended into Belgium and under the English Channel via the Channel Tunnel, or "Chunnel," to England.

Opposite: A cutaway drawing of a TGV articulated train.

Below: This detailed drawing shows the inner workings of a TGV car.

GPU pantograph

passengers/baggage compartments

auxiliary power supply unit

power pack

pneumatic block

trailer bogie

common block

main transformer

electric blocks

freon tanks

The red Belgian Thalys, modeled on the French TGV, travels back and forth to Belgium, and the blue and yellow Eurostar, operating at speeds of more than 190 mph (306 km/h), connects Brussels, London, and Paris. The TGV network also has been extended to link up with high-speed railroads in Spain and Germany. Even more lines are planned for the future.

InterCity Express

In 1968, as the French planned their TGV, West German officials from the Federal Ministry of Research and Technology, the Deutsche Bundesbahn, or German Railroad, as well as West German companies began a joint effort to research the feasibility of high-speed trains in Germany. Impressed by the efficiency and safety of the Japanese Shinkansen, German planners also were attracted by the chance to decrease the pollution caused by automobiles.

By 1970, several key decisions had been made. New high-speed rails would be laid, but they would be for both passenger and freight trains. The new lines would be the same gauge as existing lines to permit the trains to travel to smaller cities on existing rails. The new lines would be run on electric power, and German high-speed trains would follow the Japanese model of coupling cars instead of the French model of cars sharing a bogie. The basic idea was for the trains to go twice the speed of a car and half the speed of a plane, thus luring travelers out of the air and off the highway for trips that were not too long or too short.

Early plans called for existing tracks to be modified and new tracks to be laid between Cologne and Frankfurt, Hanover and Würzburg, and Munich and Hamburg. The projected cost was 12 billion deutschemarks (almost $6 billion).

Like the Japanese and the French tracks, long, welded rails were laid on top of concrete and steel ties. The builders eliminated curves wherever possible. Though the Germans and the French started building their lines at the same time, the Germans built much more slowly because of the uneven geography of Germany. In addition, the tracks in Germany had to be suitable for both passenger and freight trains. For example, unlike the French TGV lines which are only for passengers, the Germans had to build tunnels in mountainous areas to avoid climbs that were too steep for slower and heavier freight trains.

Almost twenty years of research went into the development of the InterCity Express (ICE) train itself. The West German government and independent companies, such as Siemens and Krupp, backed the research that led to the development of the ideal nose shape for the ICE as well as an onboard diagnostic system that allows quick corrections of any malfunctions. In 1988, a prototype ICE train set a world speed record of 252 mph (406 km/h) but the TGV later reclaimed this record.

The German ICE train passes over a bridge. The pantograph is clearly visible above as it gathers power from the wires overhead.

KINGDOM

London

Amsterdam

NETHERLANDS

GERMANY

Hamburg

Berlin

POLAND

Hanover

Leipzig

Dresden

Cologne

Kassel

Brussels

BELGIUM

Fulda

CZECH REP.

Frankfurt

LUXEMBOURG

Mannheim

Nuremberg

Prague

Paris

Stuttgart

Munich

Vienna

— high speed line

Singen

AUSTRIA

FRANCE

Zurich

SWITZERLAND

ICE Technology

A standard ICE-1 engine weighs 78 tons (71 t) and carries the transformer that provides the electric current for the motors that are located in the engine only. The engines, located at the front and the rear of the train, produce 7,161 horsepower of power to move the train.

Unlike Japan and France, where signaling is centrally controlled, Germany has control centers in various cities that send signals to all ICE trains and that allow for automatic braking when necessary. Because of the lack of centralized control and the different types of trains using the tracks at any given time, it is often difficult for the ICE trains to travel at their fastest speeds.

On June 2, 1991, the first ICE-1 trains began making the run between Munich and Hamburg with stops in Stuttgart, Mannheim, Frankfurt, Fulda, Kassel, and Hanover. Other lines soon followed, including lines in former East Germany. These ICE trains have sharply reduced travel time between cities.

Above: There is one stainless steel pantograph attached to each engine.

An ICE-1 train is made up of two engines and twelve cars. A standard ICE-1 train can carry 636 passengers with room to spare. Because all ICE cars are coupled, instead of sharing bogies like TGV trains, more cars can be added if needed. Like Shinkansen and TGV cars, ICE cars are sealed to prevent the air pressure from changing as the train passes through tunnels.

Bord Restaurant

In June 2000, the Germans launched their fastest high-speed train, the ICE-3. Allowed to travel at speeds up to 186 mph (299 km/h), the trains started service between Berlin and Hanover. Fifty of the eight-car trains have been ordered at a cost of $874 million. There are now more than 216 ICE-1, -2, and -3 trains available for travel.

Above: This is an example of a high-speed ICE train, which has tilting technology. It is called the ICE-T.

Unlike earlier ICEs, the ICE-3 includes motors on half of an individual car's axles. This allows the train to achieve higher speeds and accelerate more quickly than the older ICEs, which are pulled by their engines.

The amount of energy required to run the ICE-3 train as well as the amount of noise it produces also have been reduced. The most significant change, however, is that the ICE-3 is one of the first high-speed trains in Europe capable of running on all four of the different voltages used on high-speed lines in various countries. Therefore the ICE-3 can provide service across international borders.

Above, photo: The German catenary system is suspended on concrete masts, which reduces maintenance costs, and the catenary carries 15,000 volts of electricity. This is enough power for the trains to travel at almost 240 mph (387 km/h), though trains currently are allowed to travel at only 186 mph (299 km/h) for safety reasons.

Tilting Trains

Japan, France, and Germany decided to build entirely new railroad tracks that were as straight as possible to allow high-speed train travel without any passenger discomfort. Engineers in Italy, Spain, and Sweden, where train tracks often must curve through uneven countryside, discovered another way to allow trains to travel at high speeds on existing, curved track.

They realized that if the train itself could be tilted to compensate for the forces that otherwise would press passengers into their seats as a train rounded a turn at a high speed, then passengers actually would feel nothing. This would allow countries using tilting trains to avoid the high costs, environmental damage, and time required to build an entirely new high-speed rail line.

In 1971, engineers at the Fiat company in Italy developed the first working tilting train, the Pendolino, or "Little Pendulum." It got its name from its tilting motion, which as it rounded turns, caused it to move back and forth like a pendulum. In 1974, an experimental prototype Pendolino, the four-passenger car ETR 401, began test runs that eventually totaled more than 137,000 miles (220,480 km) and went on for more than six years. By the end of this test period, the train had encountered no problems in running on existing curved track.

The Pendolino, like other high-speed trains, used electric motors on each car's axles to power the train. In addition, however, the bogies carried a hydraulic device that tilted the entire car when a gyroscope sensed that the train is entering a turn. As a result, the Pendolino could run through a curve at full speed, 160 mph (257 km/h), without passengers feeling any discomfort.

This new technology requires only small changes to existing tracks. The outer rail must be ramped progressively higher so that the gyroscope can sense a curve better, and a central signaling system must be installed to ensure that drivers do not exceed safe speeds. The cost of using tilting trains is much less than the cost of building an entirely new set of tracks for other kinds of high-speed trains.

In 1988, the ETR 450 Pendolino began running between Rome and Milan, Italy, a distance of 376 miles (605 km), in just under four hours. Like the German and Japanese high-speed trains, this Pendolino train was made up of coupled individual cars.

Above: Notice how the axles are angled, in this drawing of a bogie on a tilting train car, as the train goes around a curve in the track.

Above right: This is a technical drawing, or blueprint, of the motor bogie for the Italian ETR 500.

high speed line

Milan
Verona
Venice
Turin
Genoa
Bologna
Florence
Rome
Naples

Above: A view of ETR 500

More on Tilting Trains

A modern, standard Pendolino train consists of nine cars, eight with electric motors on their axles and one a nonmotorized dining car, for a total of 480 seats. The cars are made from lightweight aluminum and the entire train weighs only 403 tons (366 t). The nine-car train is capable of producing 3,736 horsepower. The ETR 450 uses regenerative and pneumatic brakes for slowing and stopping as well as an electromagnetic emergency brake.

Although the Pendolino tilts when it goes through turns, its pantograph cannot tilt with it because it must remain in contact with the catenary that remains stationary above the train. Therefore the builders mounted the pantograph on a flexible frame anchored to the car floor which keeps it from tilting with the rest of the car.

Pendolino trains use hydraulic devices to tilt, but engineers at Talgo, a Spanish company, created a train in 1980 that uses natural forces for its tilt. The Talgo train cars are raised high on air springs, so a Talgo train tilts in the direction of the curve when it travels through it. Talgo cars share bogies, which include these high air springs. The new Talgo XXI, introduced in 1998, is capable of speeds up to 140 mph (225 km/h). The cars can be equipped with a variable gauge system, allowing the train to run on the different gauge widths of lines in France and Spain. Talgo trains currently are moved by diesel engines, but Talgo has joined with French and German companies to develop an electric engine and motorized cars.

Officials in Sweden also realized they would not be able to build new, straight rail lines. Therefore they began to develop a high-speed tilting train in the 1960s. By 1975, a prototype, the X-15, reached a speed of 150 mph (241 km/h). In the 1980s, Sweden awarded the contract to build 20 high-speed, X-2000 trains to the Asea Brown Boveri (ABB) company. The standard X-2000 train consists of one 4,400 horsepower engine at each end and five non-motorized cars in between. The whole train weighs only around 300 tons (272 t).

Tilting trains have proven very popular worldwide, especially for countries with difficult landscapes. Even Japan, France, and Germany are now either using or considering using tilting technology to improve speeds on their existing curved track.

Above: The driver's console in the new multivoltage ETR 500 cab

Below: These drawings show the front and the profile views of the new multivoltage ETR 500.

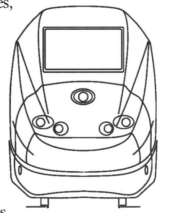

Right: This diagram explains the structure of the mechanical systems of the ETR 500.

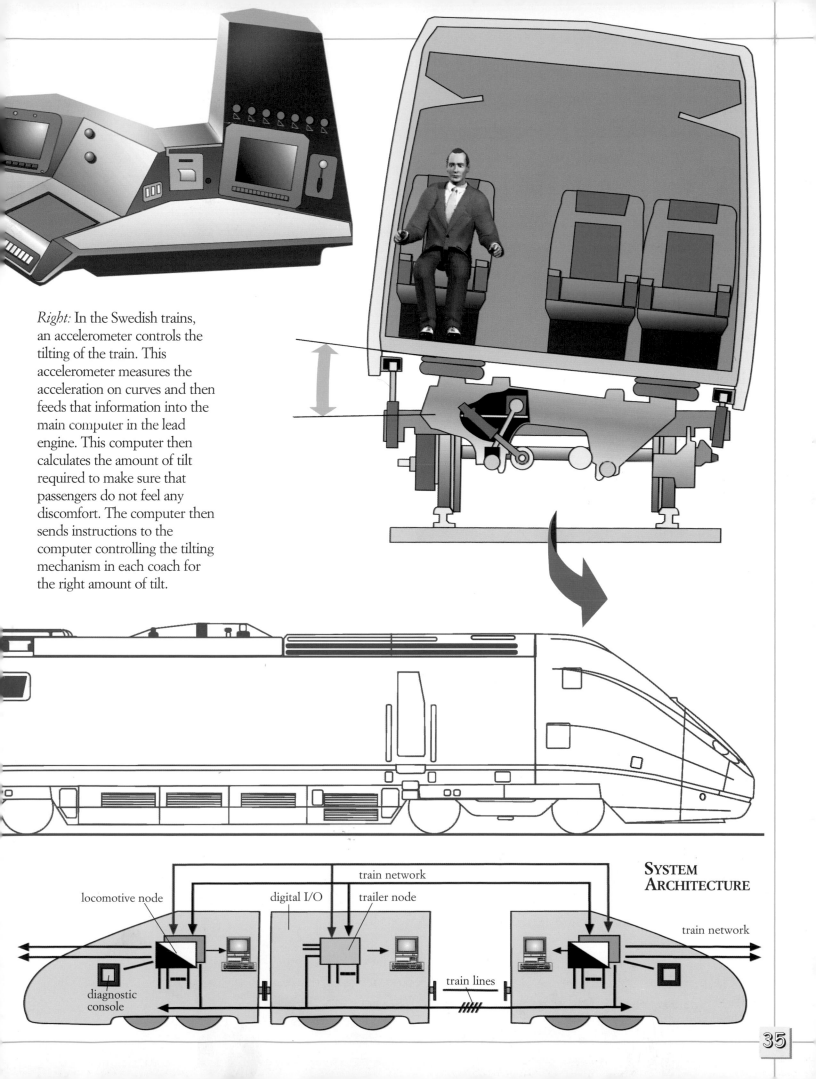

Right: In the Swedish trains, an accelerometer controls the tilting of the train. This accelerometer measures the acceleration on curves and then feeds that information into the main computer in the lead engine. This computer then calculates the amount of tilt required to make sure that passengers do not feel any discomfort. The computer then sends instructions to the computer controlling the tilting mechanism in each coach for the right amount of tilt.

SYSTEM ARCHITECTURE

train network

locomotive node

digital I/O

trailer node

train network

diagnostic console

train lines

Acela

While the rest of the world tested and developed high-speed trains, the United States was in the process of eliminating its passenger train service. Since the building of interstate highways in the 1950s, the use of passenger trains has plummeted in the United States. Only recently did U.S. officials realize that high-speed railroads in densely populated areas, such as the area between Washington D.C. and Boston, offered a cheaper alternative to either car or airplane travel. In addition, trains are much better for the environment because they consume less fuel and produce less pollution to carry more passengers than do either cars or airplanes.

Amtrak, the U.S. passenger rail carrier, is hoping to draw travelers back to the railroad by building 20 new high-speed trains. These trains run in the Northeast Corridor, a heavily populated area that includes the cities of Washington, D.C., Baltimore, Philadelphia, New York City, Providence, and Boston. This area is also known for the many curves in its existing track. Between New York and Boston, the track makes the equivalent of eleven full circles. As a result, Amtrak chose tilting technology for its high-speed train service.

In 1996, Amtrak officials awarded the design and the building of the new tilting high speed train to a team made up of Bombardier, a railroad parts manufacturer, and Alstom, the maker of the French TGV. The Bombardier-Alstom Acela, a name that combines acceleration and excellence, beat designs for an American ICE built by Siemens and an X-2000 proposed by ABB.

The Acela trains themselves consist of six cars with an engine at either end. Like the French TGV trains, cars share a bogie to reduce weight and improve aerodynamics, but this makes it difficult to either add or subtract cars. The six passenger cars also are fitted with a hydraulic tilt system. Each car tilts independently and has a tilt sensor and controller. The trains can seat 304 passengers and can allow speeds up to 150 mph (241 km/h).

The engines can produce 12,500 horsepower and can travel at speeds up to 165 mph (266 km/h). The main transformer is mounted under the floor to save space. The engines are equipped with advanced braking systems, capable of regenerative or rheostatic braking. Signals regarding speed or safety are sent directly to the driver through the rails. An Automatic Train Control system will engage the brakes if any signals are not followed. The trains also are equipped with a system that monitors power, tilting, and braking.

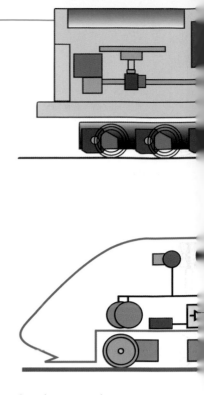

Right: These two drawings show the difference in force that a passenger feels with tilting technology and without. Without tilting technology, a passenger feels much greater force, shown by the large arrow in the drawing on the left. As shown in the drawing on the right, as the train tilts forces felt by the passenger are greatly reduced.

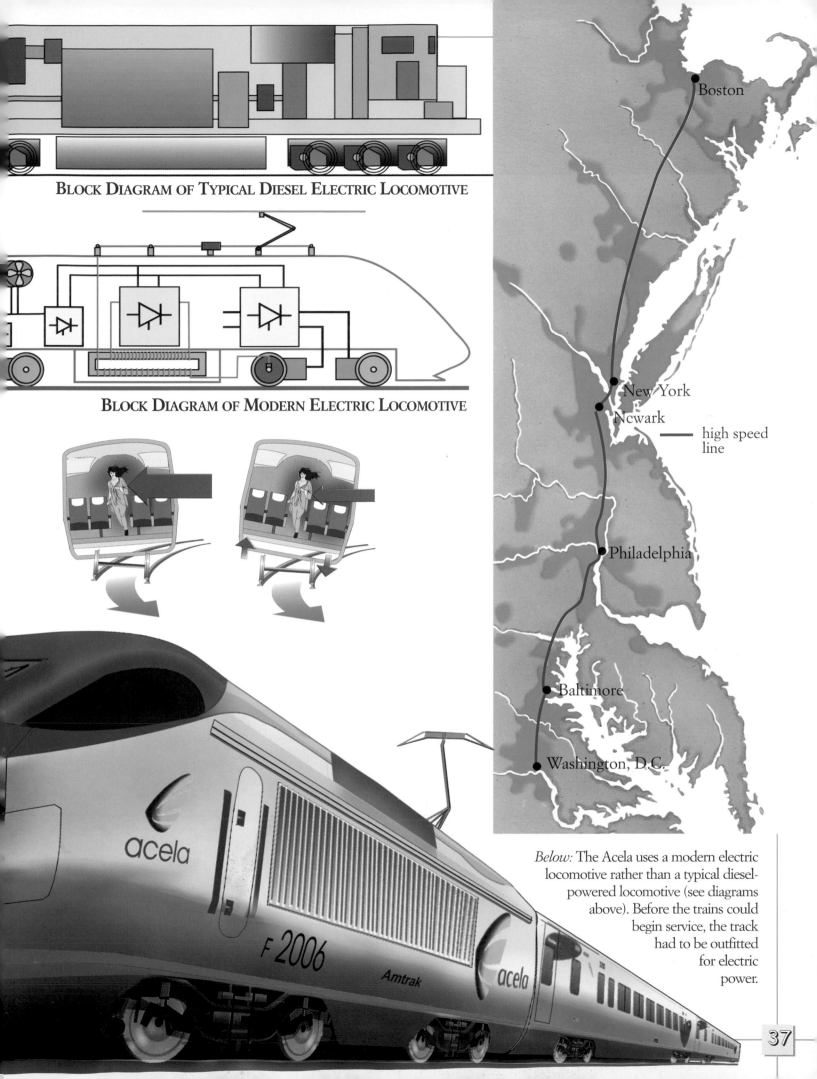

BLOCK DIAGRAM OF TYPICAL DIESEL ELECTRIC LOCOMOTIVE

BLOCK DIAGRAM OF MODERN ELECTRIC LOCOMOTIVE

Boston

New York
Newark

—— high speed
line

Philadelphia

Baltimore

Washington, D.C.

acela

F 2006

Amtrak

acela

Below: The Acela uses a modern electric
locomotive rather than a typical diesel-
powered locomotive (see diagrams
above). Before the trains could
begin service, the track
had to be outfitted
for electric
power.

Other High-Speed Lines and Worldwide Projects

The success of high-speed train service in countries like Japan, France, and Germany has led other countries to begin development of high-speed lines of their own. Among these countries are Taiwan, Spain, Australia, China, and Canada, to name a few. Some of these places had some high-speed service already, others did not, but they all are taking advantage of the technological advances in recent years to build lines that are best suited to their country's needs.

SPAIN

Following the success of the Talgo and the AVE lines that already exist in Spain, the country is planning to expand its high-speed rail service. They are working hard to standardize the lines to allow trains to run everywhere in Spain.

UNITED KINGDOM

High-speed rail service already exists between the United Kingdom, France, and Belgium. They are now considering using tilting technology to enable high-speed train service on existing conventional lines throughout the United Kingdom.

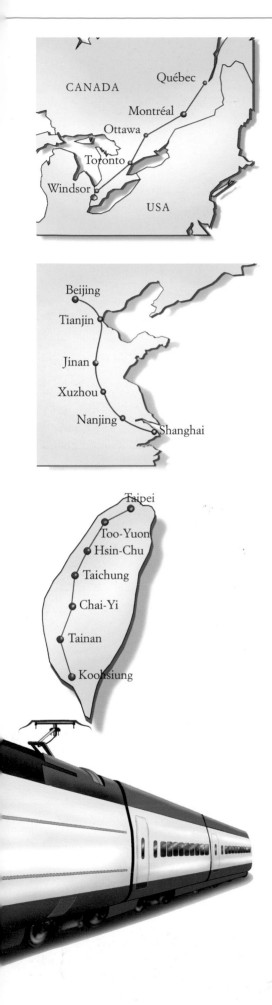

CANADA

Canada is also ready to enter the era of high-speed rail. They will use the same team that created Acela, Alstom, and Bombardier. The line is planned to travel between Quebec, Montreal, Ottawa, and Toronto at speeds up to 199 mph (320 km/h).

CHINA

With a huge population that continues to grow, the Chinese government is planning to develop a high-speed rail line that would travel between Beijing and Shanghai and reach speeds upward of 186 mph (299 km/h). The project is named Jinghu.

TAIWAN

Taiwan is building a high-speed rail service that will go a long way toward modernizing their transportation system. With the help of Seimens and Alstom they plan to have a system that covers 218 miles (351 km) and that has trains that run at speeds up to 186 mph (300 km/h).

KOREA

With a growing population and a greater volume of people using the rail service in Korea, it was decided that they needed to build a new, dedicated high-speed rail line. The Korean High Speed Rail Authority (KTRC) modeled the line after the French TGV. The line will be 256 miles (412 km) long.

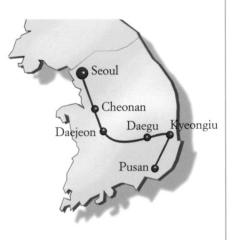

AUSTRALIA

Australia has had great success with its Queensland Rail service. It uses tilting train technology on the line that allows for speeds up to 106 mph (171 km/h). Now the Speedrail consortium, made up of Alstom and Australian construction company Leighton Contractors Pty Limited, plan to create a high-speed line that will travel between Sydney and Canberra at speeds up to 168 mph (270 km/h).

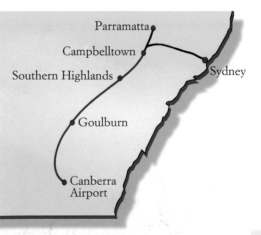

High-Speed Trains of the Future—Maglev

Throughout the world, research continues into technologies that will allow trains to travel even faster. Scientists have long speculated that the practical speed limit for steel wheels on steel rails might be 300 mph (483 km/h). This is due to several factors. First, it takes larger, heavier engines to achieve higher speeds. Second, it is difficult for pantographs to collect electricity from the catenary at higher speeds, and, third, because, at speeds more than 300 mph (483 km/h) there is a danger that the train wheels will lose contact with the rails. As a result, researchers in Japan and Germany have focused on propulsion technologies that would not require steel wheels or steel rails.

One such technology, the magnetic levitation system (maglev) is the invention of a German engineer, Hermann Kemper, who took out his first patent on the system in 1934. Further research into this idea did not take place until the 1970s. Kemper's idea was to push and pull a train down a guideway using the attractive and repulsive force of electromagnets.

As a result, maglev trains do not need engines, steering, or other controlling devices to stay on the guideway. They are much lighter than regular high-speed trains because they do not need transformers or motors. They also float on cushions of air, eliminating the friction between the trains' wheels and the rails. Without friction and with an aerodynamic design, maglev trains easily and safely can reach speeds of more than 300 mph (483 km/h).

In Germany, engineers are testing an entire maglev system, called the TransRapid. In this system, the bottom of the train wraps around a steel guideway. Electromagnets attached to the bottom of the train are directed up toward the guideway, resulting in a train that always levitates 8 millimeters (.3 inch) off the guideway. The latest prototype of this train, the TR-08, can operate at speeds up to 340 mph (547 km/h) with passengers.

In Japan, researchers are working on a competing maglev system, invented by two American scientists, James Powell and Gordon Danby. Their system is based on the repelling force of superconducting magnets. These magnets conduct electricity even after the power has been shut off, which would allow the maglev system to run with far less energy. Despite advances, problems remain. The Japanese maglev produces magnetic fields that could disrupt passengers' pacemakers or other electric devices. Japanese researchers have installed magnetic shielding in the passenger cars. The biggest problem, however, remains the huge cost involved in constructing an entirely new maglev guideway system.

The Japanese maglev train levitates nearly 4 inches (10 cm) above the guideway but must run on rubber tires until the train reaches a lift-off speed of around 60 mph (97 km/h). On April 14, 1999, a five-car prototype Japanese maglev train set a world speed record of 345 mph (555 km/h).

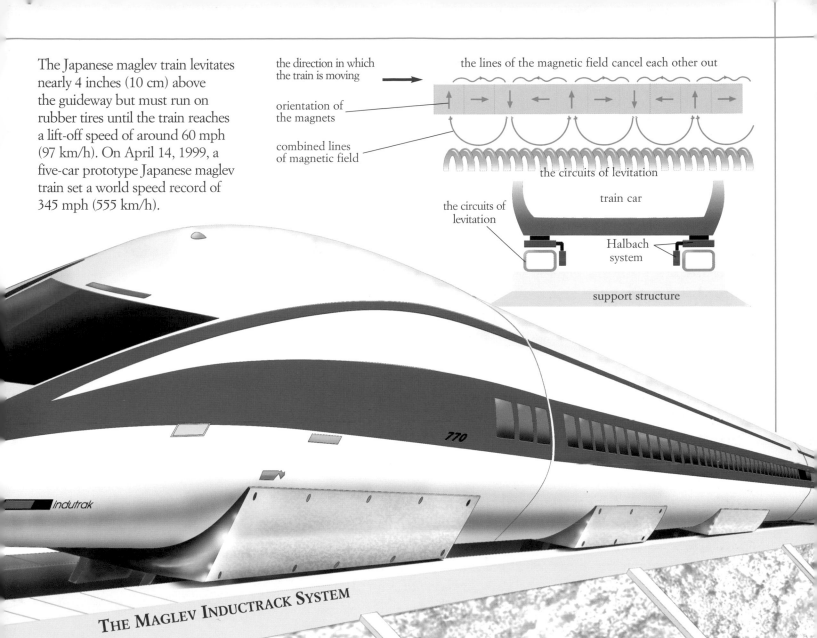

the direction in which the train is moving

the lines of the magnetic field cancel each other out

orientation of the magnets

combined lines of magnetic field

the circuits of levitation

the circuits of levitation

train car

Halbach system

support structure

THE MAGLEV INDUCTRACK SYSTEM

770

Indutrak

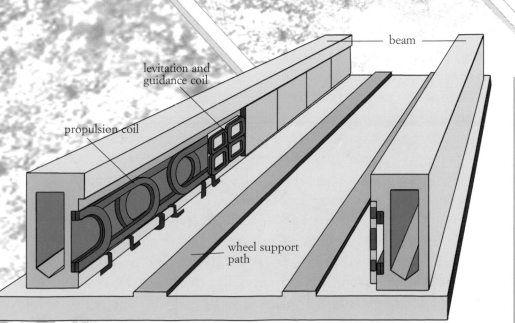

beam

levitation and guidance coil

propulsion coil

wheel support path

Right, top and bottom: Electromagnets only attract metals as long as there is an electric current running through them. In the maglev system, electrified coils built into a concrete guideway repel large magnets on the bottom of a maglev train, making the train levitate. Once the train is levitated, electricity is supplied to the coils to propel the train. The current is constantly changed back and forth so that the polarity of the magnetized coils also changes. This change in polarity causes the electromagnet in front of the train to pull it forward while the electromagnet with opposite polarity behind the train pushes it forward.

High-Speed Trains of the Future—Aerotrain

Other Japanese researchers have developed another experimental train that rides 2 to 4 inches (5–10 cm) off the ground using the Wing-in-Ground (WIG) effect. When a wing traveling at high speed approaches the ground, a funnel effect is created, increasing the air pressure and allowing the train to fly on a cushion of air while using very little energy. The same effect can be observed by dropping a piece of paper. The paper falls rapidly until it gets close to the floor, then it flattens and glides before landing.

Called the Tohuku train, or Aerotrain, this experimental train has a pair of wings in front and back with fins that tilt up. It travels in a square concrete chute with no roof. The fins stabilize the train with their own WIG effect off the walls and prevent the train from bumping into them. This double WIG effect allows the train to use even less energy.

Much testing remains to be done before a flying train could see service. Researchers must reduce the speed necessary for the train to lift off. Also, air resistance needs to be lessened so the train requires less energy to travel. According to researchers, if an Aerotrain can achieve speeds of 300 mph (483 km/h), it should be able to use about 10 times less energy than even a maglev train. At present, the train is only capable of 180 mph (290 km/h).

Nevertheless, it is possible that one day such trains will fly through their chutes powered only by solar panels on top of the walls or wind turbines lining the route. But for now, regular high-speed trains such as the Shinkansen or the TGV remain the fastest, cleanest, and cheapest way to transport passengers in highly populated areas.

Despite all the advances, much less money and time has been spent on research into improving railroad technology than on either cars or airplanes. This means that, even with all the advances covered in this book, the best high-speed train technology may not have been discovered yet.

All in all, the bullet train has come a long way, and it continues to spread throughout the world. In the future, maglev or flying trains may whisk travelers to their destination in record time while using energy provided by solar panels or wind turbines. High-speed trains truly are the transportation technology of today and tomorrow.

Below: Joining the more recent aeronautic and energetic technologies, the Japanese engineers have conceived the Aerotrain, a method of transportation that combines the advantages of the train, the airplane, and the clean energy sources of the sun and the wind.

GETS

GROUND TRANSPORTATION SYSTEM

Glossary

accelerometer (ahk-sel-uh-RAH-meh-tur) An instrument for measuring acceleration or for detecting and measuring vibrations.

Acela (ah-SEL-ah) The name, combining acceleration and excellence, chosen for the new Amtrak high-speed trains in the United States.

acid rain (AS-ihd RAYN) Raindrops filled with acid from the pollution in the air, which damage trees, lakes and rivers.

aerodynamic (ayr-oh-dy-NAM-ihk) A shape that allows air to move smoothly over an object, usually a vehicle.

air pressure (AYR PRESH-uhr) The application of force to something by the air in direct contact with it.

attractive (uh-TRAK-tiv) Having the power to pull toward itself.

axle (AK-suhl) A pin or a shaft on or around which a wheel or a set of wheels turns.

bogie (BOH-gee) A low, strongly built frame that holds two wheelsets on a train.

catenary (KAT-uh-nayr-e) A wire stretched between poles alongside high-speed train tracks that carries the electric power for the train.

combustion (kuhm-BUHS-chuhn) The burning of fuel to produce heat and light.

compensate (KOM-pen-sayt) To get rid of an undesired effect or error.

coupler (KUHP-luhr) A device on the end of a railroad car by which it links with other cars.

crank (KRANK) A bent part attached to an axle to turn it.

derail (dee-RAYL) To run off the rails.

diagnostic (dy-ig-NOS-tik) Capable of analyzing the cause or nature of a condition, situation, or problem.

diameter (di-AM-uht-uhr) The length of a straight line through the center of an object.

diesel (DEE-zuhl) A specially made form of gasoline.

dynamic brakes (dy-NAM-ik BRAYK) Advanced brakes that use motors that turn in the opposite direction of the vehicles travel to slow it down.

electromagnetic (ih-lek-troh-mag-NET-ik) Produced by an electromagnet, which is a coil of wire through which an electric current passes to create a magnet.

electromechanical (ih-lek-tro-muh-KAN-ih-kahl) A device started and controlled by electric means.

extruded (ik-STROOD-ed) Something that has been shaped by forcing through a die or other device for shaping.

feasibility (fee-zuh-BIL-iht-e) The likelihood of something being able to be done.

global warming (GLO-buhl WARM-ing) The warming of Earth's temperature due to too much pollution in the air from car exhaust and other sources.

gyroscope (JY-ruh-skohp) A wheel or disk mounted to spin rapidly around a straight shaft and capable of detecting any change in the level of that shaft.

horsepower (HORS-pow-ur) A unit of power that equals 550 feet (167 m) per pound of work per second.

hydraulic (hi-DRAH-lik) A device operated by the pressure created when liquid such as water or oil is forced through a tube or small hole.

hydrocarbon (hi-druh-KAR-buhn) A compound containing only the elements carbon and hydrogen.

install (in-STAHL) To set up for use or service.

intervals (IN-ter-vulz) The time between two events, such as two trains arriving at a station.

kilowatt (KIL-uh-wot) 1,000 watts, which are a unit used to measure power equal to the work capable of being done by an electric current in one second.

levitation (lev-uh-TA-shuhn) The act of rising and floating in the air.

malfunction (mal-FUNK-shuhn) A failure to operate in the normal way.

megalopolis (meh-guh-LAH-puh-lis) A thickly populated region between several cities.

monitor (MAHN-iht-uhr) To keep track of, regulate or control the operation of something.

Nouvelle Generation (noo-VEL JEN-uhr-ah-shi-on) Means "new generation" and refers to the advanced technologies being developed for future TGVs.

Nozomi (NO-zo-mee) "Hope," the name given to the latest shinkansen high speed trains in Japan.

obstruction (uhb-STRUHK-shuhn) Something that prevents passage, action or operation.

pantograph (PANT-uh-graf) A collapsible and adjustable pole attached to the roof of a high-speed train to draw power from the catenary for the electric motors.

Pendolino (pehn-do-LEE-no) Means "little pendulum" and refers to the tilting trains built in Italy by Fiat.

piston (PIHS-tuhn) A sliding piece in an engine moved by gas or liquid.

polarity (po-LAR-uh-tee) The particular charge, either positive or negative, of a magnet.

pneumatic (noo-MAT-ik) Moved or worked by air pressure.

propulsion (pruh-PUHL-shuhn) The action or process of driving forward by means of a force that gives motion.

prototype (PROT-uh-typ) The first full-scale and working form of a new type of a construction such as a train.

radiate (RAY-dee-ayt) To get rid of energy by sending it away.

ramped (RAMP-d) An area that has been shaped to include a slope.

regenerative braking (ree-JEH-nuh-ruh-tiv BRAYK-ing) A type of dynamic braking which turns the energy produced by braking into electric current and feeds it back into the catenary.

repulsive (ri-PUHLS-iv) Having the power to push away from itself.

rheostatic braking (RE-uh-stat-ik BRAYK-ing) A type of dynamic braking which radiates the energy produced from stopping as heat.

sensor (SEN-sor) A device that responds to heat, light, sound, pressure, magnetism or motion and transmits a resulting instruction such as for measurement or operating control.

Shinkansen (sheen-KAHN-sen) Translates as new trunk line and refers to the new tracks built to permit high speed trains to run in Japan.

smog (SMOG) A dirty fog made by the action of the sun's rays on hydrocarbons from car exhaust in the air.

superconductivity (soo-per-kahn-duhk-TIV-ih-tee) The ability to allow an electric current to pass through without losing any energy. Currently possible only at extremely cold temperatures.

suspension (suh-SPEN-shuhn) The system of devices, such as springs, supporting the upper part of a vehicle on the axles.

switch (SWICH) A device made of two movable rails designed to turn a train from one track to another.

Talgo (TAL-go) The name of the company and the tilting trains it produces in Spain.

technology (tek-NAH-luh-jee) The tools and science used to create objects and machines for human use.

Thalys (TAL-ees) The name of the red Belgian TGV.

Glossary

tie (TY) A rectangular piece of wood, stone or steel on the ground to which railroad rails are fastened to keep them in line and stable (also known as a sleeper).

traction (TRAK-shuhn) The friction of an object, such as a train wheel, on the surface on which it moves that keeps the object in place.

Train à Grande Vitesse (TREHN A GRAHND vee-TESS) Translates as high speed train and refers to the tracks, system and trains that comprise the high speed train system in France.

transformer (trans-FOR-muhr) A device which converts variations of current from one circuit into a specific voltage and current in a second circuit.

turbine (TER-bin) A rotary engine that moves by the action of a current of fluid such as water, steam, gas, or air.

variable (VAYR-e-uh-buhl) Something that changes regularly.

ventilation (ven-tuh-LAY-shuhn) A system or means of providing fresh air.

viaduct (VI-uh-duhkt) A short bridge that carries a road or railroad over an obstruction, such as another road or valley.

voltage (VOL-tij) The amount of electric current measured in volts.

Wing-in-Ground (WIG) **effect** (WING IN GRAUND i-FEKT) A high pressure cushion of air that forms from the funnel created when a wing of a flying vehicle gets very close to the ground.

welded (WELD-ed) Metallic parts that have been joined by heating, allowing them to flow together.

Additional Resources

To learn more about bullet trains check out the following books and Web sites.

Books
Cant, Christopher. *High Speed Trains.* Chelsea House, 1999.

Cefrey, Holly. *High Speed Trains: Built for Speed.* Children's Press, 2000.

Herring, Peter. *Ultimate Train.* DK Publishing, Inc., 2000.

Web Site
www.trainweb.com

Index

A
Acela, 6, 36, 39
Aerotrain, 42
Alstom, 36, 39
Amtrak, 36
Asea Brown Boveri (ABB) company, 34

B
bogie(s), 12, 14, 26, 28
Bombardier, 36, 39
brakes, 14–15, 24, 26, 30, 34, 36

C
catenary(ies), 12, 14, 22, 24, 34, 40
"Chunnel," 27

D
Daishimizu tunnel, 20
Danby, Gordon, 40
Diesel, Rudolf, 8
diesel engine, 12
Deutsche Bundesbahn, 28

E
electric engine(s), 12, 22
electric motor(s), 18, 27, 32, 34
ETR-450 Pendolino, 32

F
Fiat company, 32

I
ICE-1 trains, 30
ICE-3 trains, 30–31
InterCity Express (ICE), 10, 28, 30

J
Japanese National Railways, 16
Joetsu Shinkansen, 20

K
Kemper, Hermann, 40
Korean High Speed Rail Authority (KTRC), 39
Krupp, 28

L
Leighton Contractors Pty Limited, 39

M
magnetic levitation train (maglev), 6, 40, 42

N
New Castle, 8
noise, 19, 21–22, 31
Northeast Corridor, 6, 36
Nozomi series, 20–21

P
pantograph, 26, 34
Pendolino, 32–33
Powell, James, 40

Q
Queensland Rail service, 39

R
Rocket, 8

S
Sanyo Shinkansen, 19–20
Shinkansen, 10, 12, 14, 16, 18–22, 24, 26, 28, 42
Siemens & Halske, 8, 28, 36, 39
slabtrack, 14
Société National des Chemins de Fer Français(SNCF), 22
Sogo, Shinji, 16
Speedrail consortium, 39
Stephenson, George, 8

T
Talgo, 34
Talgo XXI, 34, 38
TGV Atlantique (TGV-A), 24, 27
TGV Nouvelle Génération (TGV-NG), 27
TGV Sud-Est (TGV-SE), 24
tilting trains, 32–36
Tohuku Shinkansen, 19
Tokaido Shinkansen line, 16, 20, 24
Train à Grande Vitesse (TGV), 10, 12, 14, 22, 24, 26, 28, 42
TransRapid, 40
Trevithick, Richard, 8

V
ventilation system, 18

W
Wing-in-Ground effect (WIG), 42

About the Author

David Biello is a writer and editor living in New York City. He has spent the last four years covering environmental developments in transportation, government, and even finance. He has also had the good fortune to ride many of the high-speed trains covered in this book, including the TGV, ICE, and Acela.

Photo Credits